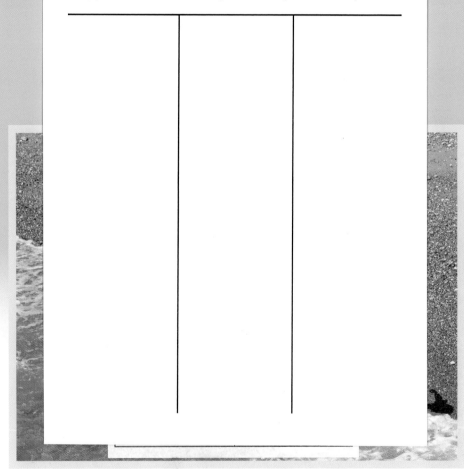

Written by Sally Hewitt

Photography by Chris Fairclough

W

FRANKLIN WATTS
LONDON • SYDNEY

Always go for a walk with an adult. Take care around water.

First published in 2005 by
Franklin Watts
96 Leonard Street,
London EC2A 4XD

Franklin Watts Australia
45-51 Huntley Street,
Alexandria, NSW 2015

© Franklin Watts 2005

Editors: Caryn Jenner, Sarah Ridley
Designer: Louise Best
Art director: Jonathan Hair
Photography: Chris Fairclough
Map: Hardlines

Many thanks to Jemma, Emmie and Iola Collins
and Harry Jandula for agreeing to appear in
the book.

A CIP catalogue record for this book is
available from the British Library

ISBN 0 7496 6039 2

Printed in China

Contents

High tide

The weather is just right
for a walk by the sea.
The sun is shining.
A breeze is blowing.

The tide is high.
The sea splashes on the pebbles.
Wooden breakwaters protect
the beach from the waves.

Paddling

You can take off
your shoes
and paddle in
the shallow
water.

The waves break
on the beach
and make the
water white and
foamy.

The water's edge

A line of seaweed lies along
the water's edge.

Waves push the pebbles up the beach and make a slope. Why is it hard work running up the shingle?

Looking at the horizon

A sign points over the sea to France.
France is too far away to see ...

... even through a telescope.

The sea and the sky meet on the horizon.

On the promenade

A kiosk on the promenade sells food, drink and beach toys.

Colourful windmills spin in the breeze.

Who would you send a postcard to?

It is shady on the bandstand.
The band isn't playing today.

The pier

The pier stretches out to sea.
People fish off the end of the pier.

From the pier, you can look back towards land.

Houses and hotels line the seafront.

Why do you think there is a lifebelt on the pier?

The sea wall

A sea wall protects the town.
Waves pound against it in
stormy weather.

Fish and chips make a delicious lunch.
Perhaps one of these fishing boats caught the fish.

Low tide

The tide is going out.
Now you can see seaweed and
barnacles clinging to the breakwaters
higher up the beach.

You can run faster on the wet sand than on the pebbles.

What has made these patterns on the sand?

Sailing

A sea breeze blows off the water.
Hold onto your hats!

Sailors in wet suits get their boat
ready to sail.
Why is it a good day for sailing?

Beach huts

A row of beach huts stands at the top of the beach. You can store useful things in a beach hut.

It is a good place to rest after a long walk by the sea.

Map

You can start a walk from any point on a map. To follow the walk in this book, put your finger on **Start** and trace the route.

Key

beach hut

bandstand

car park

breakwater

hotel

fishing boat

pier

putting green

sea wall

shop

sign

telescope

Quiz

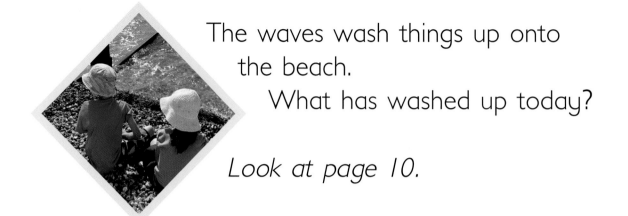

The waves wash things up onto the beach.
What has washed up today?

Look at page 10.

You can buy postcards at the kiosk.
What else can you buy?

Look at page 14.

You can walk along the pier.
What else can you do on the pier?

Look at pages 16 and 17.

The beach is on one side of the
sea wall.
What is on the other side?

Look at page 18.

Breakwaters protect the beach.
What clings onto the
breakwaters?

Look at page 20.

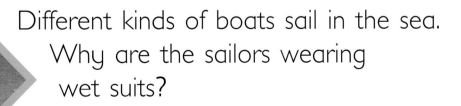

Different kinds of boats sail in the sea.
Why are the sailors wearing
wet suits?

Look at page 23.

Index